Old-Fashioned
Christmas
Cookies

PiL

Publications International, Ltd.
Favorite Brand Name Recipes at www.fbnr.com

Microwave Cooking: Microwave ovens vary in wattage. Use the cooking times as guidelines and check for doneness before adding more time.

Preparation/Cooking Times: Preparation times are based on the approximate amount of time required to assemble the recipe before cooking, baking, chilling or serving. These times include preparation steps such as measuring, chopping and mixing. The fact that some preparations and cooking can be done simultaneously is taken into account. Preparation of optional ingredients and serving suggestions is not included.

Contents

Christmas Classics

Crispy Thumbprint Cookies

1 package (18.25 ounces) yellow cake mix
½ cup vegetable oil
¼ cup water
1 egg
3 cups crisp rice cereal, crushed
½ cup chopped walnuts
Raspberry or strawberry preserves

Preheat oven to 375°F. Combine cake mix, oil, water and egg. Beat until well blended. Add cereal and walnuts; mix until well blended. Drop by heaping teaspoonfuls about 2 inches apart onto ungreased baking sheets. Use thumb to make indentation in each cookie. Spoon about ½ teaspoon preserves into center of each cookie. Bake 9 to 11 minutes or until golden brown. Cool cookies 1 minute on baking sheet; remove to wire rack to cool completely.

Makes 3 dozen cookies

Tiny Mini Kisses Peanut Blossoms

¾ **cup REESE'S® Creamy Peanut Butter**
½ **cup shortening**
⅓ **cup granulated sugar**
⅓ **cup packed light brown sugar**
1 **egg**
3 **tablespoons milk**
1 **teaspoon vanilla extract**
1½ **cups all-purpose flour**
½ **teaspoon baking soda**
½ **teaspoon salt**
 Granulated sugar
 HERSHEY'S MINI KISSES™ Semi-Sweet *or*
 Milk Chocolate Baking Pieces

1. Heat oven to 350°F.

2. Beat peanut butter and shortening in large bowl with electric mixer until well mixed. Add ⅓ cup granulated sugar and brown sugar; beat well. Add egg, milk and vanilla; beat until fluffy. Stir together flour, baking soda and salt; gradually add to peanut butter mixture, beating until blended. Shape into ½-inch balls. Roll in granulated sugar; place on ungreased cookie sheet.

3. Bake 5 to 6 minutes or until set. Immediately press Mini Kiss™ into center of each cookie. Remove from cookie sheet to wire rack.
Makes about 14 dozen cookies

Holiday Peppermint Slices

1 **package (18 ounces) refrigerated sugar**
 cookie dough
¼ **teaspoon peppermint extract, divided**
 Red food coloring
 Green food coloring

1. Remove dough from wrapper according to package directions. Cut dough into thirds.

2. Combine ⅓ of dough, ⅛ teaspoon peppermint extract and enough red food coloring to make dough desired shade of red. Beat until evenly tinted.

3. Repeat with second ⅓ of dough, remaining ⅛ teaspoon peppermint extract and green food coloring.

4. To assemble, shape each portion of dough into 8-inch roll. Place red roll beside green roll; press together slightly. Place plain roll on top. Press rolls together to form one tri-colored roll; wrap in plastic wrap. Refrigerate 2 hours or overnight.

5. Preheat oven to 350°F.

6. Cut dough into ¼-inch-thick slices. Place 2 inches apart on ungreased cookie sheets. Bake 8 to 9 minutes or until set but not browned. Cool 1 minute on cookie sheets. Cool completely on wire racks.
Makes 2½ dozen cookies

Tiny Mini Kisses Peanut Blossoms

Candy Cane & Wreath Ornaments

1 cup sugar
½ cup shortening
½ cup butter, softened
1 teaspoon salt
1 egg
2 teaspoons vanilla
2½ cups all-purpose flour
½ teaspoon almond extract
¼ teaspoon liquid green food coloring
¼ teaspoon peppermint extract
½ teaspoon liquid red food coloring, divided
   Decorator's Frosting (recipe follows)
   Assorted red candies

1. Beat sugar, shortening, butter and salt in large bowl until light and fluffy. Beat in egg and vanilla until well blended. Beat in flour until soft dough forms. Remove half of dough from bowl; set aside. Divide remaining dough evenly between 2 medium bowls. Stir almond extract and green food coloring into one portion until well blended. Stir peppermint extract and ¼ teaspoon red food coloring into remaining portion until well blended.

2. Place level teaspoonfuls of each dough on large baking sheet. Cover; refrigerate 15 minutes or until slightly firm.

3. Preheat oven to 375°F. Place 1 teaspoon red dough, 1 teaspoon green dough and 2 teaspoons uncolored dough on lightly floured surface. Roll out each portion into 6- to 7-inch rope with lightly floured hands. Place 1 green rope next to 1 uncolored rope and 1 red rope next to remaining uncolored rope. Twist each pair of ropes together 7 or 8 times; place on ungreased baking sheet.

4. Shape red and white rope into candy cane and green and white rope into wreath. Repeat with remaining dough.

5. Bake 7 to 9 minutes or until cookies are firm. *Do not allow to brown.* Transfer cookies with spatula to wire racks; cool completely.

6. Prepare Decorator's Frosting. Tint half of frosting with remaining ¼ teaspoon red food coloring. Spoon frostings into decorating bags fitted with writing tips. Pipe cluster of berries onto wreaths with red frosting. Glue candies onto wreaths with white frosting. Let stand 1 hour or until icing is set. Tie ribbon loops or bows onto each cookie.   *Makes 4 dozen cookies*

Decorator's Frosting

1½ cups vegetable shortening
1½ teaspoons lemon, coconut, almond or
      peppermint extract
7½ cups sifted powdered sugar
⅓ cup milk

Beat shortening and extract in large bowl until fluffy. Slowly add half of sugar, ½ cup at a time, beating well after each addition. Beat in milk. Add remaining sugar; beat 1 minute more until smooth and fluffy. Store in refrigerator.

Makes about 5 cups

Candy Cane & Wreath Ornaments

Original Nestlé® Toll House® Chocolate Chip Cookies

2¼ cups all-purpose flour
1 teaspoon baking soda
1 teaspoon salt
1 cup (2 sticks) butter, softened
¾ cup granulated sugar
¾ cup packed brown sugar
1 teaspoon vanilla extract
2 eggs
2 cups (12-ounce package) NESTLÉ® TOLL HOUSE® Semi-Sweet Chocolate Morsels
1 cup chopped nuts

COMBINE flour, baking soda and salt in small bowl. Beat butter, granulated sugar, brown sugar and vanilla in large mixer bowl. Add eggs, one at a time, beating well after each addition. Gradually beat in flour mixture. Stir in morsels and nuts. Drop by rounded tablespoon onto ungreased baking sheets.

BAKE in preheated 375°F. oven for 9 to 11 minutes or until golden brown. Cool on baking sheets for 2 minutes; remove to wire racks to cool completely.
Makes about 5 dozen cookies

Pan Cookie Variation: PREPARE dough as above. Spread into greased 15½×10½-inch jelly-roll pan. Bake in preheated 375°F. oven for 20 to 25 minutes or until golden brown. Cool in pan on wire rack. Makes 4 dozen bars.

Slice and Bake Cookie Variation: PREPARE dough as directed. Divide in half; wrap in wax paper. Chill for 1 hour or until firm. Shape each half into 15-inch log; wrap in wax paper. Chill for 30 minutes.* Cut into ½-inch-thick slices; place on ungreased baking sheets. Bake in preheated 375°F. oven for 8 to 10 minutes or until golden brown. Cool on baking sheets for 2 minutes; remove to wire racks to cool completely. Makes about 5 dozen cookies.*

May be stored in refrigerator for up to 1 week or in freezer for up to 8 weeks.

Chocolate Chip Macaroons

2½ cups flaked coconut
⅔ cup mini semisweet chocolate chips
⅔ cup sweetened condensed milk
1 teaspoon vanilla

Preheat oven to 350°F. Grease cookie sheets. Combine coconut, chocolate chips, milk and vanilla in medium bowl; mix until well blended. Drop dough by rounded teaspoonfuls 2 inches apart onto greased cookie sheets. Press dough gently with back of spoon to flatten slightly. Bake 10 to 12 minutes or until light golden brown. Let cookies stand on cookie sheets 1 minute. Remove cookies to wire racks; cool completely.
Makes about 3½ dozen cookies

Original Nestlé® Toll House® Chocolate Chip Cookies

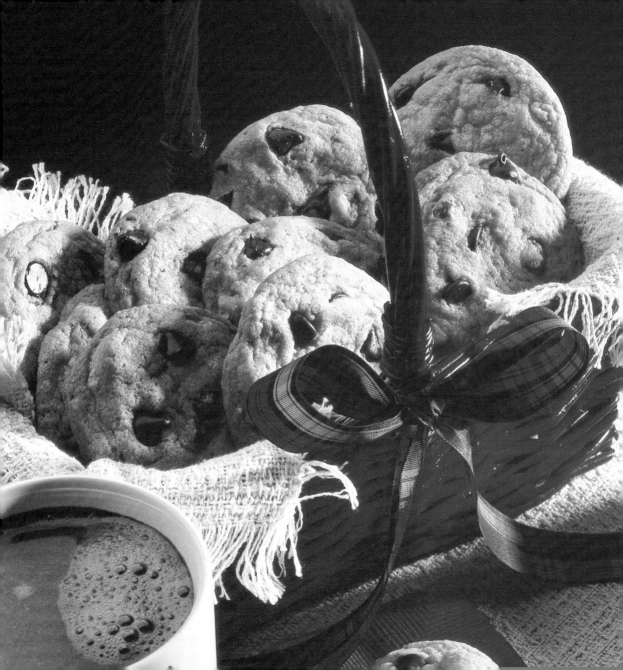

Chocolate-Dipped Almond Horns

1½ cups powdered sugar
1 cup butter, softened
2 egg yolks
1½ teaspoons vanilla
2¼ cups all-purpose flour
½ cup ground almonds
1 teaspoon cream of tartar
1 teaspoon baking soda
2 cups semisweet chocolate chips, melted
Powdered sugar

1. Preheat oven to 325°F. In large bowl, combine powdered sugar and butter. Beat at medium speed, scraping bowl often, until creamy, 1 to 2 minutes.

2. Add egg yolks and vanilla; continue beating until well blended, 1 to 2 minutes.

3. Reduce speed to low. Add flour, almonds, cream of tartar and baking soda. Continue beating, scraping bowl often, until well mixed, 1 to 2 minutes.

4. Shape into 1-inch balls. Roll balls into 2½-inch ropes; shape into crescents. Place 2 inches apart on ungreased cookie sheets.

5. Bake 8 to 10 minutes or until set. (Cookies do not brown.) Cool completely.

6. Dip half of each cookie into chocolate; sprinkle remaining half with powdered sugar. Refrigerate until set. *Makes about 3 dozen cookies*

Lemony Butter Cookies

½ cup butter, softened
½ cup sugar
1 egg
1½ cups all-purpose flour
1 teaspoon grated lemon peel
2 tablespoons fresh lemon juice
½ teaspoon baking powder
⅛ teaspoon salt
Additional sugar

Beat butter and sugar in large bowl with electric mixer until creamy. Beat in egg until light and fluffy. Mix in flour, lemon peel and juice, baking powder and salt. Cover; refrigerate about 2 hours or until firm.

Preheat oven to 350°F. Roll out dough, small portion at a time, on well-floured surface to ¼-inch thickness. (Keep remaining dough in refrigerator.) Cut with 3-inch round cookie cutter. Transfer to ungreased cookie sheets. Sprinkle with sugar.

Bake 8 to 10 minutes or until lightly browned on edges. Cool 1 minute on cookie sheets. Remove to wire racks; cool completely. Store in airtight container. *Makes about 2½ dozen cookies*

Belgian Tuile Cookies

½ cup butter, softened
½ cup sugar
1 large egg white
1 teaspoon vanilla
¼ teaspoon salt
½ cup all-purpose flour
4 ounces bittersweet chocolate, chopped

1. Preheat oven to 375°F. Grease cookie sheets; set aside.

2. Beat butter and sugar in large bowl until light and fluffy. Beat in egg white, vanilla and salt. Gradually add flour. Beat until well blended. Drop rounded teaspoonfuls of batter 4 inches apart onto prepared cookie sheets. Flatten slightly with spatula.

3. Bake 6 to 8 minutes or until cookies are deep golden brown. Let cookies stand on cookie sheet 1 minute. Working quickly, while cookies are still hot, drape cookies over rolling pin or bottle so both sides hang down and form saddle shape; cool completely.

4. Melt chocolate in small, heavy saucepan over low heat, stirring constantly. Tilt saucepan to pool chocolate at one end; dip edge of each cookie, turning slowly so entire edge is tinged with chocolate.

5. Transfer cookies to waxed paper; let stand at room temperature 1 hour or until set. Store tightly covered at room temperature. Do not freeze.

Makes about 2½ dozen cookies

Pfeffernüsse

3½ cups all-purpose flour
2 teaspoons baking powder
1½ teaspoons ground cinnamon
1 teaspoon ground ginger
½ teaspoon baking soda
½ teaspoon salt
½ teaspoon ground cloves
½ teaspoon ground cardamom
¼ teaspoon black pepper
1 cup butter, softened
1 cup granulated sugar
¼ cup dark molasses
1 egg
Powdered sugar

Combine flour, baking powder, cinnamon, ginger, baking soda, salt, cloves, cardamom and pepper in large bowl.

Beat butter and sugar in large bowl until light and fluffy. Beat in molasses and egg. Gradually add flour mixture. Beat until dough forms. Shape dough into disk; wrap in plastic wrap and refrigerate until firm, 30 minutes or up to 3 days.

Preheat oven to 350°F. Grease cookie sheets. Roll dough into 1-inch balls. Place 2 inches apart on prepared cookie sheets.

Bake 12 to 14 minutes or until golden brown. Transfer cookies to wire racks; dust with sifted powdered sugar. Cool completely. Store tightly covered at room temperature or freeze up to 3 months.

Makes about 5 dozen cookies

Pumpkin White Chocolate Drops

2 cups butter, softened
2 cups granulated sugar
1 can (16 ounces) solid pack pumpkin
2 eggs
4 cups all-purpose flour
2 teaspoons pumpkin pie spice
1 teaspoon baking powder
½ teaspoon baking soda
1 bag (12 ounces) white chocolate chips
1 container (16 ounces) ready-to-spread
    cream cheese frosting
¼ cup packed brown sugar

1. Preheat oven to 375°F. Grease cookie sheets.

2. Beat butter and granulated sugar in large bowl until light and fluffy. Add pumpkin and eggs; beat until smooth. Add flour, pumpkin pie spice, baking powder and baking soda; beat just until well blended. Stir in chips.

3. Drop dough by teaspoonfuls about 2 inches apart onto prepared cookie sheets. Bake about 16 minutes or until set and bottoms are brown. Cool 1 minute on cookie sheets. Remove to wire rack to cool.

4. Combine frosting and brown sugar in small bowl. Spread on warm cookies.

Makes about 6 dozen cookies

Swedish Cookie Shells

1 cup butter, softened
⅔ cup sugar
1 large egg white
1 teaspoon vanilla
½ teaspoon almond extract
2 cups all-purpose flour, divided
¼ cup finely ground blanched almonds

1. Beat butter and sugar in large bowl until light and fluffy. Beat in egg white, vanilla and almond extract until well blended. Gradually add 1½ cups flour and almonds. Beat until well blended. Stir in enough remaining flour with spoon to form soft dough. Form dough into 1-inch-thick square; wrap in plastic wrap and refrigerate until firm, 1 hour or overnight.

2. Preheat oven to 375°F. Press rounded teaspoonfuls of dough into greased sandbakelser tins or mini muffin pan cups. Place tins on baking sheet. Bake 8 to 10 minutes or until cookie shells are lightly browned. Cool cookies in tins 1 minute.

3. Carefully loosen cookies from tins with point of small knife. Invert tins over wire racks; tap lightly to release cookies; cool completely (cookies should be shell-side up). Repeat with remaining dough; cool cookie tins between batches.

4. Serve cookies shell-side up. Store tightly covered at room temperature or freeze up to 3 months.

Makes about 10 dozen cookies

Pumpkin White Chocolate Drops

Christmas Spritz Cookies

2¼ cups all-purpose flour
¼ teaspoon salt
1¼ cups powdered sugar
1 cup butter, softened
1 large egg
1 teaspoon vanilla
1 teaspoon almond extract
Green food coloring (optional)
Candied red and green cherries and
   assorted decorative candies (optional)
Icing (recipe follows, optional)

Preheat oven to 375°F. Place flour and salt in medium bowl; stir to combine. Beat powdered sugar and butter in large bowl. Beat in egg, vanilla and almond extract. Gradually add flour mixture. Beat at low speed until well blended.

Divide dough in half. If desired, tint half of dough green with food coloring. Fit cookie press with desired plate (or change plates for different shapes after first batch). Fill press with dough; press dough 1 inch apart onto ungreased cookie sheets. Decorate cookies with cherries and assorted candies, if desired.

Bake 10 to 12 minutes or until just set. Remove cookies to wire racks; cool completely.

Prepare Icing, if desired. Pipe or drizzle on cooled cookies. Decorate with cherries and assorted candies, if desired. Store tightly covered at room temperature or freeze up to 3 months.

Makes about 5 dozen cookies

Icing

1½ cups powdered sugar
2 tablespoons milk plus additional, if
   needed
⅛ teaspoon almond extract

Place all ingredients in medium bowl; stir until thick, but spreadable. (If icing is too thick, stir in 1 teaspoon additional milk.)

Golden Kolacky

½ cup butter, softened
4 ounces cream cheese, softened
1 cup all-purpose flour
Fruit preserves

Combine butter and cream cheese in large bowl; beat until smooth. Gradually add flour to butter mixture, blending until mixture forms soft dough. Divide dough in half; wrap each half in plastic wrap. Refrigerate until firm.

Preheat oven to 375°F. Roll out dough, half at a time, on floured surface to ⅛-inch thickness. Cut into 3-inch squares. Spoon 1 teaspoon preserves in center of each square. Bring up two opposite corners to center; pinch together tightly to seal. Fold sealed tip to one side; pinch to seal. Place 1 inch apart on ungreased cookie sheets. Bake 10 to 15 minutes or until lightly browned. Remove to racks; cool completely.

Makes about 2½ dozen cookies

Christmas Spritz Cookies

Danish Lemon-Filled Spice Cookies (Medaljekager)

2¼ cups all-purpose flour
1 teaspoon ground cinnamon
½ teaspoon ground allspice
½ teaspoon ground ginger
½ teaspoon ground nutmeg
¼ teaspoon salt
1 large egg yolk
¾ cup butter, softened
¾ cup sugar
¼ cup milk
1 teaspoon vanilla
Lemon Filling (recipe follows)

Grease cookie sheets; set aside. Place flour, cinnamon, allspice, ginger, nutmeg and salt in medium bowl; stir to combine. Place egg yolk in large bowl; add butter, sugar, milk and vanilla. Beat butter mixture with electric mixer at medium speed until light and fluffy. Gradually add flour mixture. Beat at low speed until dough forms. Cover dough and refrigerate 30 minutes or until firm.

Preheat oven to 350°F. Roll teaspoonfuls of dough into ½-inch balls; place 2 inches apart on prepared cookie sheets. Flatten each ball to ¼-inch thickness with bottom of glass dipped in sugar. Prick top of each cookie using fork. Bake 10 to 13 minutes or until golden brown. Remove cookies to wire racks; cool completely.

Prepare Lemon Filling. Spread filling on flat side of half of cookies. Top with remaining cookies, pressing flat sides together. Let stand at room temperature until set. Store tightly covered at room temperature or freeze up to 3 months.

Makes about 3 dozen sandwich cookies

Lemon Filling

2¼ cups sifted powdered sugar
3 tablespoons lemon juice
1½ tablespoons butter, softened
½ teaspoon lemon extract

Beat all ingredients in medium bowl with electric mixer at medium speed until smooth.

Makes about 1 cup

Danish Lemon-Filled Spice Cookies (Medaljekager)

Heavenly Bars

Fudge-Filled Bars

1 (14-ounce) can EAGLE® BRAND Sweetened Condensed Milk
   (NOT evaporated milk)
1 (12-ounce) package semi-sweet chocolate chips
2 tablespoons butter or margarine
2 teaspoons vanilla extract
2 (18-ounce) packages refrigerated cookie dough (oatmeal-chocolate
   chip, chocolate chip, or sugar cookie dough)

Preheat oven to 350°F. In heavy saucepan over medium heat, combine **Eagle Brand,** chips and butter; heat until chips melt, stirring often. Remove from heat; stir in vanilla. Cool 15 minutes. Using floured hands, press 1½ packages of cookie dough into ungreased 15×10×1-inch baking pan. Pour cooled chocolate mixture evenly over dough. Crumble remaining dough over filling. Bake 25 to 30 minutes. Cool. Cut into bars. Store covered at room temperature.

Makes 48 bars

Chocolate Cherry Bars

1 cup (2 sticks) butter or margarine
¾ cup HERSHEY'S Cocoa or HERSHEY'S
    Dutch Processed Cocoa
2 cups sugar
4 eggs
1½ cups plus ⅓ cup all-purpose flour, divided
⅓ cup chopped almonds
1 can (14 ounces) sweetened condensed
    milk (not evaporated milk)
½ teaspoon almond extract
1 cup HERSHEY'S MINI KISSES™ Semi-
    Sweet or Milk Chocolate Baking Pieces
1 cup chopped maraschino cherries,
    drained

1. Heat oven to 350°F. Generously grease 13×9×2-inch baking pan.

2. Melt butter in large saucepan over low heat; stir in cocoa until smooth. Remove from heat. Add sugar, 3 eggs, 1½ cups flour and almonds; mix well. Pour into prepared pan. Bake 20 minutes.

3. Meanwhile, whisk together remaining 1 egg, remaining ⅓ cup flour, sweetened condensed milk and almond extract. Pour over baked layer; sprinkle Mini Kisses™ and cherries over top. Return to oven.

4. Bake additional 20 to 25 minutes or until set and edges are golden brown. Cool completely in pan on wire rack. Refrigerate until cold, 6 hours or overnight. Cut into bars. Cover; refrigerate leftover bars. *Makes about 48 bars*

Butterscotch Brownies

1 cup butterscotch chips
½ cup packed light brown sugar
¼ cup butter, softened
2 eggs
½ teaspoon vanilla
1 cup all-purpose flour
½ teaspoon baking powder
¼ teaspoon salt
1 cup semisweet chocolate chips

Preheat oven to 350°F. Grease 9-inch square baking pan. Melt butterscotch chips in small saucepan over low heat, stirring constantly; set aside.

Beat sugar and butter in large bowl until light and fluffy. Beat in eggs, one at a time, scraping down side of bowl after each addition. Beat in melted butterscotch chips and vanilla. Combine flour, baking powder and salt in small bowl; add to butter mixture. Beat until well blended. Spread batter evenly in prepared pan.

Bake 20 to 25 minutes or until golden brown and center is set. Remove pan from oven and immediately sprinkle with chocolate chips. Let stand about 4 minutes or until chocolate is melted. Spread chocolate evenly over top. Place pan on wire rack; cool completely. Cut into 2¼-inch squares. *Makes about 16 brownies*

Chocolate Cherry Bars

Festive Fruited White Chip Blondies

½ cup (1 stick) butter or margarine
1⅔ cups (10-ounce package) HERSHEY₁S
    Premier White Chips, divided
2 eggs
¼ cup granulated sugar
1¼ cups all-purpose flour
⅓ cup orange juice
¾ cup cranberries, chopped
¼ cup chopped dried apricots
½ cup coarsely chopped nuts
¼ cup packed light brown sugar

1. Heat oven to 325°F. Grease and flour 9-inch square baking pan.

2. Melt butter in medium saucepan; stir in 1 cup white chips. In large bowl, beat eggs until foamy. Add granulated sugar; beat until thick and pale yellow in color. Add flour, orange juice and white chip mixture; beat just until combined. Spread one-half of batter, about 1¼ cups, into prepared pan.

3. Bake 15 minutes until edges are lightly browned; remove from oven.

4. Stir cranberries, apricots and remaining ⅔ cup white chips into remaining one-half of batter; spread over top of hot baked mixture. Stir together nuts and brown sugar; sprinkle over top.

5. Bake 25 to 30 minutes or until edges are lightly browned. Cool completely in pan on wire rack. Cut into bars.   *Makes about 16 bars*

Cinnamony Apple Streusel Bars

1¼ cups graham cracker crumbs
1¼ cups all-purpose flour
¾ cup packed brown sugar, divided
¼ cup granulated sugar
1 teaspoon ground cinnamon
¾ cup butter, melted
2 cups chopped apples (2 medium apples, cored and peeled)
Glaze (recipe follows)

Preheat oven to 350°F. Grease 13×9-inch baking pan. Combine graham cracker crumbs, flour, ½ cup brown sugar, granulated sugar, cinnamon and melted butter in large bowl until well blended; reserve 1 cup. Press remaining crumb mixture into bottom of prepared pan. Bake 8 minutes. Remove from oven; set aside.

Toss apples with remaining ¼ cup brown sugar in medium bowl until brown sugar is dissolved; arrange apples over baked crust. Sprinkle reserved 1 cup crumb mixture over filling. Bake 30 to 35 minutes more or until apples are tender. Remove pan to wire rack; cool completely. Drizzle with Glaze. Cut into bars.   *Makes 3 dozen bars*

Glaze

Combine ½ cup powdered sugar and 1 tablespoon milk in small bowl until well blended.

Festive Fruited White Chip Blondies

Lemon Nut Bars

1⅓ cups all-purpose flour
½ cup firmly packed brown sugar
¼ cup granulated sugar
¾ cup butter or margarine
1 cup old-fashioned or quick oats, uncooked
½ cup chopped nuts
1 package (8 ounces) PHILADELPHIA®
   Cream Cheese, softened
1 egg
1 tablespoon grated lemon peel
3 tablespoons lemon juice

PREHEAT oven to 350°F.

STIR together flour and sugars in medium bowl. Cut in butter until mixture resembles coarse crumbs. Stir in oats and nuts. Reserve 1 cup crumb mixture; press remaining crumb mixture onto bottom of greased 13×9-inch baking pan. Bake 15 minutes.

BEAT cream cheese, egg, lemon peel and juice in small mixing bowl at medium speed with electric mixer until well blended. Pour over crust; sprinkle with reserved crumb mixture.

BAKE 25 minutes. Cool in pan on wire rack. Cut into bars. *Makes about 3 dozen bars*

Kickin' Brownies

½ cup hazelnuts or unblanched almonds
¾ cup butter
2 cups sugar
¾ cup cocoa powder
3 eggs, lightly beaten
2 teaspoons vanilla
1 cup all-purpose flour
1½ cups fresh or thawed frozen raspberries
   White Ganache (recipe follows)
   Chocolate Ganache (recipe follows)
3 to 4 tablespoons raspberry jam

1. Preheat oven to 350°F. To remove skins from nuts, spread in single layer on baking sheet. Bake 10 to 12 minutes or until skins begin to flake off; cool slightly. Wrap hazelnuts in heavy kitchen towel; rub against towel to remove as much of skins as possible. Cool completely. Place hazelnuts in food processor. Process using on/off pulsing action until hazelnuts are finely chopped, but not pasty. Set aside.

2. Lightly grease 2 (8-inch) square baking pans. Line bottoms of pans with foil; lightly grease foil. Set aside.

3. Melt butter in medium saucepan over medium heat, stirring occasionally. Remove saucepan from heat. Stir in sugar and cocoa powder until well blended. Stir in eggs and vanilla until smooth. Stir in flour just until blended. Pour batter evenly into prepared pans. Place raspberries on top of batter, pressing gently into batter.

4. Bake 15 to 20 minutes or until center is just set. *Do not overbake.* Cool brownies completely in pans on wire rack.

5. Run knife around edges of pans to loosen brownies from sides. Gently work flexible metal spatula down edges and slightly under brownies to loosen from bottoms of pans. Hold wire rack over top of 1 pan; invert to release brownie. Remove foil; discard. Place cutting board or plate over brownie; invert brownie.

6. Prepare White Ganache and Chocolate Ganache. Reserve 2 tablespoons White Ganache; spread remaining White Ganache evenly over brownie. Spread raspberry jam on top of ganache.

7. Unmold remaining brownie as directed in Step 5. Place flat-side down on bottom layer, pressing gently to seal. Spread Chocolate Ganache evenly over top layer. Drizzle reserved 2 tablespoons White Ganache over top. Sprinkle with hazelnuts. Cut into 16 squares. Store tightly covered in refrigerator.
Makes 16 brownies

White Ganache

 **1 cup (6 ounces) white chocolate chips or
    chopped white chocolate, divided**
 3 tablespoons whipping cream
 ½ teaspoon almond extract

1. Combine ½ cup chocolate and whipping cream in medium saucepan. Heat over medium heat until chocolate is half melted, stirring occasionally.

2. Remove saucepan from heat. Stir in remaining ½ cup chocolate and almond extract until mixture is smooth. Keep warm (ganache is semi-firm at room temperature). *Makes ¾ cup*

Chocolate Ganache

 2 tablespoons whipping cream
 1 tablespoon butter
 **½ cup (2 ounces) semisweet chocolate chips
    or chopped semisweet chocolate**
 ½ teaspoon vanilla

1. Combine whipping cream and butter in small saucepan. Heat over medium heat until mixture boils, stirring frequently.

2. Remove saucepan from heat. Stir in chocolate and vanilla until mixture is smooth, returning to heat for 20 to 30 second intervals as needed to melt chocolate. Keep warm (ganache is semi-firm at room temperature). *Makes ¾ cup*

Three Great Tastes Blond Brownies

2 cups packed light brown sugar
1 cup (2 sticks) butter or margarine, melted
2 eggs
2 teaspoons vanilla extract
2 cups all-purpose flour
1 teaspoon salt
⅔ cup (of each) HERSHEY₅S Semi-Sweet Chocolate Chips, REESE'S₅ Peanut Butter Chips, and HERSHEY₅S Premier White Chips
Chocolate Chip Drizzle (recipe follows)

1. Heat oven to 350°F. Grease 15½×10½×1-inch jelly-roll pan.

2. Stir together brown sugar and butter in large bowl; beat in eggs and vanilla until smooth. Add flour and salt, beating just until blended; stir in chocolate, peanut butter and white chips. Spread batter into prepared pan.

3. Bake 25 to 30 minutes or until wooden pick inserted in center comes out clean. Cool completely in pan on wire rack. Cut into bars. With tines of fork, drizzle Chocolate Chip Drizzle randomly over bars. *Makes about 72 bars*

Chocolate Chip Drizzle

In small microwave-safe bowl, place ¼ cup HERSHEY₅S Semi-Sweet Chocolate Chips and ¼ teaspoon shortening (do not use butter, margarine, spread or oil). Microwave at HIGH (100%) 30 seconds to 1 minute; stir until chips are melted and mixture is smooth.

Chocolate Dream Bars

½ cup butter, softened
1½ cups packed light brown sugar, divided
1 egg yolk
1 cup plus 2 tablespoons all-purpose flour
2 eggs
1 cup (6 ounces) semi-sweet chocolate chips
½ cup chopped toasted walnuts

Preheat oven to 375°F. Grease 13×9-inch baking pan. Cream butter with ½ cup sugar and egg yolk in large bowl until light and well blended. Stir in 1 cup flour until well blended. Press dough on bottom of prepared pan. Bake 12 to 15 minutes or until golden. Meanwhile, beat remaining 1 cup sugar, 2 tablespoons flour and whole eggs in same bowl until light and frothy. Spread mixture over hot baked crust. Return to oven; bake about 15 minutes or until topping is set. Remove from oven; sprinkle with chocolate chips. Let stand until chips melt; spread chips evenly over bars. Sprinkle with walnuts. Cool in pan on wire rack. Cut into 2×1-inch bars. *Makes about 5 dozen bars*

Three Great Tastes Blond Brownies

Magic Cookie Bars

½ cup (1 stick) butter or margarine
1½ cups graham cracker crumbs
1 (14-ounce) can EAGLE® BRAND
    Sweetened Condensed Milk
    (NOT evaporated milk)
2 cups (12 ounces) semi-sweet chocolate
    chips
1⅓ cups flaked coconut
1 cup chopped nuts

1. Preheat oven to 350°F (325°F for glass dish). In 13×9-inch baking pan, melt butter in oven.

2. Sprinkle crumbs over butter; pour **Eagle Brand** evenly over crumbs. Layer evenly with remaining ingredients; press down firmly.

3. Bake 25 minutes or until lightly browned. Cool. Chill if desired. Cut into bars. Store loosely covered at room temperature.   *Makes 24 to 36 bars*

7-Layer Magic Cookie Bars: Substitute 1 cup (6 ounces) butterscotch-flavored chips* for 1 cup semi-sweet chocolate chips and proceed as directed above.

Peanut butter-flavored chips or white chocolate chips may be substituted for butterscotch-flavored chips.

Magic Rainbow Cookie Bars: Substitute 2 cups plain candy-coated chocolate candies for semi-sweet chocolate chips and proceed as directed above.

Chewy Toffee Almond Bars

1 cup (2 sticks) butter, softened
½ cup sugar
2 cups all-purpose flour
1¾ cups (10-ounce package) SKOR® English
    Toffee Bits or HEATH® Bits 'O Brickle™
    Almond Toffee Bits
¾ light corn syrup
1 cup sliced almonds, divided
¾ cup MOUNDS® Sweetened Coconut Flakes,
    divided

1. Heat oven to 350°F. Grease sides of 13×9×2-inch baking pan.

2. Beat butter and sugar until fluffy. Gradually add flour, beating until well blended. Press dough evenly into prepared pan.

3. Bake 15 to 20 minutes or until edges are lightly browned. Meanwhile, combine toffee bits and corn syrup in medium saucepan. Cook over medium heat, stirring constantly, until toffee is melted (about 10 to 12 minutes). Stir in ½ cup almonds and ½ cup coconut. Spread toffee mixture to within ¼-inch of edges of crust. Sprinkle remaining ½ cup almonds and remaining ¼ cup coconut over top.

4. Bake an additional 15 minutes or until bubbly. Cool completely in pan on wire rack. Cut into bars.
    Makes about 36 bars

Top to bottom: 7-Layer Magic Cookie Bars and Magic Rainbow Cookie Bars

Chocolate Nut Bars

½ **cup uncooked quick oats**
½ **cup hazelnuts, chopped**
½ **cup walnuts, chopped**
¾ **cup powdered sugar**
8 **ounces (1¼ cups) semisweet chocolate chips**
1 **tablespoon vegetable shortening**
2 **tablespoons butter**
½ **teaspoon salt**
⅓ **cup corn syrup**
½ **teaspoon vanilla**

1. Preheat oven to 350°F. Line 8-inch square baking pan with foil, pressing foil into corners to cover completely and leaving 1-inch overhang on sides.

2. Spread oats on ungreased baking sheet. Bake 8 to 10 minutes or until light golden brown. Let cool; place in large bowl. *Reduce oven temperature to 325°F.* Spread hazelnuts and walnuts on ungreased baking sheet. Bake 9 to 11 minutes or just until cut sides begin to brown lightly. Let cool; add to toasted oats. Stir in powdered sugar; set aside.

3. Heat chocolate chips and shortening in heavy small saucepan over very low heat, stirring constantly, until melted and smooth. Remove from heat. Spread evenly onto bottom of prepared pan. Let stand in cool place 15 to 20 minutes or until it begins to set, but is not firm.

4. Combine butter and salt in microwavable bowl. Microwave at HIGH 45 to 55 seconds or until butter is melted and foamy. Stir in corn syrup; let cool slightly and add vanilla. Stir corn syrup mixture into oat mixture just until moistened. Gently spoon over chocolate, spreading evenly into corners. Score lightly into 4 strips, then score each strip into 6 pieces. Cover tightly with plastic wrap and refrigerate until firm, at least 4 hours.

5. Remove from pan by lifting foil by edges. Place on cutting board; cut along score lines into 24 pieces. Remove from foil. Store in airtight container in refrigerator. *Makes 24 bars*

Chocolate Nut Bars

Irresistible Chocolate

Chewy Chocolate Macaroons

5⅓ cups MOUNDS® Sweetened Coconut Flakes
½ cup HERSHEY'S Cocoa
1 can (14 ounces) sweetened condensed milk (not evaporated milk)
2 teaspoons vanilla extract
About 24 red candied cherries, halved (optional)

1. Heat oven to 350°F. Generously grease cookie sheet.

2. Stir together coconut and cocoa in large bowl; stir in sweetened condensed milk and vanilla until well blended. Drop by rounded teaspoons onto prepared cookie sheet. Press cherry half into center of each cookie, if desired.

3. Bake 8 to 10 minutes or until almost set. Immediately remove from cookie sheet to wire rack. Cool completely. Store loosely covered at room temperature.

Makes about 4 dozen cookies

Chocolate Almond Biscotti

½ cup (1 stick) butter or margarine, softened
1¼ cups sugar
2 eggs
1 teaspoon almond extract
2¼ cups all-purpose flour
¼ cup HERSHEY₅S Dutch Processed Cocoa
   or HERSHEY₅S Cocoa
1 teaspoon baking powder
¼ teaspoon salt
1 cup sliced almonds
   Chocolate Glaze (recipe follows)
   White Glaze (recipe follows)
   Additional sliced almonds (optional)

1. Heat oven to 350°F. Beat butter and sugar until blended. Add eggs and almond extract; beat well. Stir together flour, cocoa, baking powder and salt; gradually add to butter mixture, beating until smooth. (Dough will be thick.) Stir in almonds using wooden spoon.

2. Shape dough into two 11-inch-long rolls. Place rolls 3 to 4 inches apart on large ungreased cookie sheet.

3. Bake 30 minutes or until rolls are set. Remove from oven; cool on cookie sheet 15 minutes. Using serrated knife, cut rolls diagonally using sawing motion, into ½-inch-thick slices. Arrange slices, cut sides down, close together on cookie sheet.

4. Bake 8 to 9 minutes. Turn slices over; bake an additional 8 to 9 minutes. Remove from oven; cool on cookie sheet on wire rack. Prepare Chocolate Glaze. Dip end of each biscotti in glaze or drizzle over entire cookie. Prepare White Glaze; drizzle over chocolate glaze. Garnish with additional almonds, if desired.

Makes about 2½ dozen cookies

Chocolate Glaze

Place 1 cup HERSHEY₅S Semi-Sweet Chocolate Chips and 1 tablespoon shortening (do not use butter, margarine or oil) into small microwave-safe bowl. Microwave at HIGH (100%) 1 to 1½ minutes or until smooth when stirred. Makes about 1 cup glaze.

White Glaze

Place ¼ cup HERSHEY₅S Premier White Chips and 1 teaspoon shortening (do not use butter, margarine or oil) into small microwave-safe bowl. Microwave at HIGH (100%) 30 to 45 seconds or until smooth when stirred. Makes about ¼ cup glaze.

Prep Time: 30 minutes
Bake Time: 46 minutes
Cool Time: 1 hour

Chocolate Almond Biscotti

Chocolate-Raspberry Kolacky

2 squares (1 ounce each) semisweet chocolate, coarsely chopped
1½ cups all-purpose flour
¼ teaspoon baking soda
¼ teaspoon salt
½ cup butter, softened
3 ounces cream cheese or light cream cheese, softened
⅓ cup granulated sugar
1 teaspoon vanilla
   Seedless raspberry jam
   Powdered sugar

Place chocolate in microwavable 1-cup glass measure. Microwave at HIGH (100% power) 1 to 2 minutes or until chocolate is melted, stirring after 1 minute.

Combine flour, baking soda and salt in small bowl; stir well. Beat butter and cream cheese in large bowl with electric mixer at medium speed until well blended. Beat in granulated sugar until light and fluffy. Beat in vanilla and chocolate. Gradually add flour mixture. Beat at low speed just until blended. Divide dough in half; flatten each half into a disc. Wrap separately in plastic wrap. Refrigerate 1 to 2 hours or until firm.

Preheat oven to 375°F. Lightly grease cookie sheets. Roll out each dough disc on well-floured surface to ¼- to ⅛-inch thickness. Cut out with 3-inch round cookie cutter. Place 2 inches apart on prepared cookie sheets. Place rounded ½ teaspoon jam in center of each circle. Bring three edges of dough circles up over jam; pinch edges together to seal, leaving center of triangle slightly open.

Bake 10 minutes or until set. Let cookies stand on cookie sheets 2 minutes. Remove cookies with spatula to wire racks; cool completely. Just before serving, sprinkle with powdered sugar. Store tightly covered in refrigerator; let stand for 30 minutes at room temperature before serving.

Makes about 1½ dozen cookies

Note: These cookies do not freeze well.

Chocolate-Raspberry Kolacky Cups: Fit dough circles into greased mini-muffin cups; fill with heaping teaspoon of jam. Bake 10 minutes or until set. Let pans stand on wire racks; cool completely. Dust with powdered sugar before serving.

Chocolate-Raspberry Kolacky

White Chocolate Chunk & Macadamia Nut Brownie Cookies

1½ cups firmly packed light brown sugar
⅔ CRISCO® Stick or ⅔ cup CRISCO®
    all-vegetable shortening
1 tablespoon water
1 teaspoon vanilla
2 eggs
1½ cups all-purpose flour
⅓ cup unsweetened cocoa powder
½ teaspoon salt
¼ teaspoon baking soda
1 cup white chocolate chunks or chips
1 cup coarsely chopped macadamia nuts

1. Heat oven to 375°F. Place sheets of foil on countertop for cooling cookies.

2. Place brown sugar, ⅔ cup shortening, water and vanilla in large bowl. Beat at medium speed of electric mixer until well blended. Add eggs; beat well.

3. Combine flour, cocoa, salt and baking soda. Add to shortening mixture; beat at low speed just until blended. Stir in white chocolate and nuts.

4. Drop dough by rounded measuring tablespoonfuls 2 inches apart onto ungreased baking sheet.

5. Bake one baking sheet at a time at 375°F for 7 to 9 minutes or until cookies are set. *Do not overbake.* Cool 2 minutes on baking sheet. Remove cookies to foil to cool completely.
Makes about 3 dozen cookies

Cocoa-Walnut Crescents

1 cup margarine
⅔ cup powdered sugar
⅓ cup unsweetened cocoa
1 teaspoon vanilla extract
⅛ teaspoon salt
1⅔ cups all-purpose flour
1 cup PLANTERS® Walnuts, finely chopped
    Powdered Sugar Glaze (recipe follows)
    and chopped PLANTERS® Walnuts, for
    garnish

1. Beat margarine and sugar in large bowl with mixer at medium speed until light and fluffy. Blend in cocoa, vanilla and salt. Mix in flour and finely chopped walnuts. Wrap; refrigerate 1 hour.

2. Shape rounded teaspoons of dough into crescent shapes, tapering ends. Place on lightly greased baking sheets.

3. Bake in preheated 325°F oven for 15 to 18 minutes. Remove from sheets; cool completely on wire racks. Drizzle with Powdered Sugar Glaze and sprinkle with chopped walnuts, if desired.
Makes 4 dozen cookies

Powdered Sugar Glaze

Combine 1 cup powdered sugar and 5 to 6 teaspoons water.

Cocoa-Walnut Crescents

Triple Chocolate Pretzels

2 squares (1 ounce each) unsweetened chocolate
½ cup butter, softened
½ cup granulated sugar
1 egg
2 cups cake flour
1 teaspoon vanilla
¼ teaspoon salt
Mocha Glaze (recipe follows)
2 ounces white chocolate, chopped

Melt unsweetened chocolate in top of double boiler over hot, not boiling, water. Remove from heat; cool. Cream butter and granulated sugar in large bowl until light. Add egg and melted chocolate; beat until fluffy. Stir in cake flour, vanilla and salt until well blended. Cover; refrigerate until firm, about 1 hour.

Preheat oven to 400°F. Lightly grease cookie sheets or line with parchment paper. Divide dough into 4 equal parts. Divide each part into 12 pieces. To form pretzels, knead each piece briefly to soften dough. Roll into rope about 6 inches long. Form each rope on prepared cookie sheet into pretzel shape. Repeat with all pieces of dough, spacing cookies 2 inches apart. Bake 7 to 9 minutes or until firm. Remove to wire racks to cool.

Prepare Mocha Glaze. Dip pretzels, one at a time, into glaze to coat completely. Place on waxed paper, right side up. Let stand until glaze is set.

Melt white chocolate in small bowl over hot water. Squeeze melted chocolate through pastry bag or drizzle over pretzels to decorate. Let stand until chocolate is completely set.

Makes 4 dozen cookies

Mocha Glaze

1 cup (6 ounces) semisweet chocolate chips
1 teaspoon light corn syrup
1 teaspoon shortening
1 cup powdered sugar
3 to 5 tablespoons hot coffee or water

Combine chocolate chips, corn syrup and shortening in small heavy saucepan. Stir over low heat until chocolate is melted. Stir in powdered sugar and enough coffee to make a smooth glaze.

Baker's® Chocolate Sugar Cookies

2 cups all-purpose flour
1 teaspoon baking soda
¼ teaspoon salt
3 squares BAKER'S® Unsweetened Baking Chocolate
1 cup (2 sticks) butter *or* margarine
1 cup sugar
1 egg
1 teaspoon vanilla
   Additional sugar

HEAT oven to 375°F. Mix flour, baking soda and salt in medium bowl.

MICROWAVE chocolate and butter in large microwavable bowl on HIGH 2 minutes or until butter is melted. Stir until chocolate is completely melted.

STIR 1 cup sugar into melted chocolate mixture until well blended. Mix in egg and vanilla until completely blended. Stir in flour mixture until well blended. Refrigerate dough about 15 minutes or until easy to handle.

SHAPE dough into 1-inch balls; roll in additional sugar. Place on ungreased cookie sheets.

BAKE 8 to 10 minutes or until set. (If flatter, crisper cookies are desired, flatten with bottom of glass before baking.) Remove from cookie sheets. Cool on wire racks. Store in tightly covered container.

Makes about 3½ dozen cookies

Melting Chocolate on Top of Stove: Melt chocolate and butter in 3-quart heavy saucepan on low heat; stir constantly until chocolate is just melted. Remove from heat. Continue as directed.

Jam-Filled Chocolate Sugar Cookies: Prepare Baker's® Chocolate Sugar Cookie dough as directed. Roll in finely chopped nuts in place of sugar. Make indentation in each ball; fill center with your favorite jam. Bake as directed.

Chocolate-Caramel Sugar Cookies: Prepare Baker's® Chocolate Sugar Cookie dough as directed. Roll in finely chopped nuts in place of sugar. Make indentation in each ball; bake as directed. Microwave 1 package (14 ounces) KRAFT® Caramels with 2 tablespoons milk in microwavable bowl on HIGH 3 minutes or until melted, stirring after 2 minutes. Fill centers of cookies with caramel mixture. Drizzle with melted Baker's® Semi-Sweet Chocolate.

Prep Time: 20 minutes plus refrigerating
Bake Time: 10 minutes

Chocolate Almond Cookies

1 cup (2 sticks) butter or margarine, softened
1 cup sugar
1 egg
½ teaspoon almond extract
½ teaspoon vanilla extract
2 cups all-purpose flour
½ cup HERSHEY'S Cocoa
¼ teaspoon baking powder
¼ teaspoon baking soda
⅛ teaspoon salt
1 cup HERSHEY'S MINI CHIPS™ Semi-Sweet
   Chocolate
Additional sugar
Slivered blanched almonds

1. Beat butter and 1 cup sugar in large bowl until fluffy. Add egg, almond and vanilla extracts; beat well. Combine flour, cocoa, baking powder, baking soda and salt; gradually add to butter mixture, beating to form smooth dough. Stir in small chocolate chips. If necessary, refrigerate dough about 1 hour or until firm enough to handle.

2. Heat oven to 350°F. Shape dough into 1⅛-inch balls; roll in sugar. Place about 2 inches apart on ungreased cookie sheet. Place three slivered almonds on top of each ball; press slightly.

3. Bake 9 to 10 minutes or until set. Cool slightly. Remove from cookie sheet to wire rack. Cool completely.   *Makes about 3½ dozen cookies*

Chocolate Cherry Cookies

½ cup (1 stick) butter, softened
½ cup sugar
1 egg
2 squares (1 ounce each) unsweetened
   chocolate, melted and cooled
2 cups cake flour
1 teaspoon vanilla
¼ teaspoon salt
   Maraschino cherries, well drained
   (about 48)
1 cup semi-sweet or milk chocolate chips

Beat butter and sugar in large bowl until light. Add egg and melted chocolate; beat until fluffy. Stir in cake flour, vanilla and salt until well blended. Cover; refrigerate until firm, about 1 hour.

Preheat oven to 400°F. Lightly grease cookie sheets or line with parchment paper. Shape dough into 1-inch balls. Place 2 inches apart on prepared cookie sheets. With knuckle of finger, make deep indentation in center of each ball. Place cherry into each indentation. Bake 8 minutes or just until set. Meanwhile, melt chocolate chips in small bowl over hot water. Stir until melted. Remove cookies to wire racks. Drizzle melted chocolate over tops of cookies while still warm. Refrigerate cookies until chocolate is set.

Makes about 4 dozen cookies

Chocolate Almond Cookies

Cinnamon Nut Chocolate Spirals

1½ cups all-purpose flour
¼ teaspoon salt
⅓ cup butter, softened
¾ cup sugar, divided
1 egg
1 cup mini semisweet chocolate chips
1 cup very finely chopped walnuts
2 teaspoons ground cinnamon
3 tablespoons butter

Combine flour and salt in small bowl; set aside. Beat softened butter and ½ cup sugar in large bowl with electric mixer at medium speed until light and fluffy. Beat in egg. Gradually add flour mixture. Dough will be stiff. (If necessary, knead dough by hand until it holds together.)

Roll out dough between 2 sheets of waxed paper into 12×10-inch rectangle. Remove waxed paper from top of rectangle.

Combine chips, walnuts, remaining ¼ cup sugar and cinnamon in medium bowl. Melt 3 tablespoons butter; pour hot melted butter over chocolate chip mixture; mix well. (Chips will partially melt.) Spoon mixture over dough. Spread evenly, leaving ½-inch border on long edges.

Using bottom sheet of waxed paper as guide and starting at long side, tightly roll up dough jelly-roll style, removing waxed paper as you roll. Wrap in plastic wrap; refrigerate 30 minutes to 1 hour.

Preheat oven to 350°F. Lightly grease cookie sheets. Unwrap dough. Using heavy thread or dental floss, cut dough into ½-inch slices. Place slices 2 inches apart on prepared cookie sheets.

Bake 14 minutes or until edges are light golden brown. Cool completely on wire racks.

Makes about 2 dozen cookies

Chocolate Spritz

2 squares (1 ounce each) unsweetened chocolate
1 cup butter, softened
½ cup granulated sugar
1 egg
1 teaspoon vanilla
¼ teaspoon salt
2¼ cups all-purpose flour
Powdered sugar

Preheat oven to 400°F. Line cookie sheets with parchment paper or leave ungreased. Melt chocolate in top of double boiler over hot, not boiling, water. Remove from heat; cool. Beat butter, granulated sugar, egg, vanilla and salt in large bowl until light. Blend in melted chocolate and flour until stiff. Fit cookie press with your choice of plate. Load press with dough; press cookies out onto cookie sheets, spacing 2 inches apart.

Bake 5 to 7 minutes or just until very slightly browned around edges. Remove to wire racks to cool. Sprinkle with powdered sugar.

Makes about 5 dozen cookies

Cinnamon Nut Chocolate Spirals

Festive Fruits & Nuts

Cashew-Lemon Shortbread Cookies

- ½ **cup roasted cashews**
- 1 **cup butter, softened**
- ½ **cup sugar plus additional**
- 2 **teaspoons lemon extract**
- 1 **teaspoon vanilla**
- 2 **cups all-purpose flour**

Preheat oven to 325°F. Place cashews in food processor; process until finely ground. Add butter, ½ cup sugar, lemon extract and vanilla; process until well blended. Add flour; process using on/off pulsing action until dough is well blended and begins to form a ball. Shape dough into 1½-inch balls; roll in additional sugar. Place about 2 inches apart on ungreased baking sheets; flatten. Bake cookies 17 to 19 minutes or just until set and edges are lightly browned. Remove cookies from baking sheets to wire rack to cool.

Makes 2 to 2½ dozen cookies

 50

Ultimate Chocolate Chip Cookies

1¼ cups firmly packed brown sugar
¾ Butter Flavor* CRISCO® Stick or ¾ cup
    Butter Flavor CRISCO® all-vegetable
    shortening
2 tablespoons milk
1 tablespoon vanilla
1 egg
1¾ cups all-purpose flour
1 teaspoon salt
¾ teaspoon baking soda
1 cup semisweet chocolate chips
1 cup coarsely chopped pecans**

Butter Flavor Crisco is artificially flavored.
**You may substitute an additional ½ cup semisweet chocolate chips for pecans.*

1. Heat oven to 375°F. Place sheets of foil on countertop for cooling cookies.

2. Combine sugar, ¾ cup shortening, milk and vanilla in large bowl. Beat at medium speed of electric mixer until well blended. Beat in egg.

3. Combine flour, salt and baking soda. Mix into shortening mixture at low speed just until blended. Stir in chocolate chips and nuts.

4. Drop by rounded tablespoonfuls 3 inches apart onto ungreased baking sheets.

5. Bake at 375°F for 8 to 10 minutes for chewy cookies or 11 to 13 minutes for crisp cookies. *Do not overbake.* Cool 2 minutes on baking sheets. Remove to foil to cool completely.

Makes 3 dozen cookies

Pecan Mini Kisses Cups

½ cup (1 stick) butter or margarine, softened
1 package (3 ounces) cream cheese,
    softened
1 cup all-purpose flour
1 egg
⅔ cup packed light brown sugar
1 tablespoon butter, melted
1 teaspoon vanilla extract
    Dash salt
72 HERSHEY®S MINI KISSES™ Milk Chocolate
    Baking Pieces, divided
½ to ¾ cup coarsely chopped pecans

1. Beat ½ cup softened butter and cream cheese in medium bowl until blended. Add flour; beat well. Cover; refrigerate about 1 hour or until firm enough to handle.

2. Heat oven to 325°F. Stir together egg, brown sugar, 1 tablespoon melted butter, vanilla and salt in small bowl until well blended.

3. Shape chilled dough into 24 balls (1 inch each). Place balls in ungreased small muffin cups (1¾ inches in diameter). Press onto bottoms and up sides of cups. Place 2 Mini Kisses™ in each cup. Spoon about 1 teaspoon pecans over chocolate. Fill each cup with egg mixture.

4. Bake 25 minutes or until filling is set. Lightly press 1 Mini Kiss™ into center of each cookie. Cool in pan on wire rack.   *Makes 24 cups*

Ultimate Chocolate Chip Cookies

Double-Dipped Hazelnut Crisps

¾ **cup semisweet chocolate chips**
1¼ **cups all-purpose flour**
¾ **cup powdered sugar**
⅔ **cup whole hazelnuts, toasted, hulled and**
  finely ground*
¼ **teaspoon instant espresso powder**
  Dash salt
½ **cup butter, softened**
2 **teaspoons vanilla**
4 **squares (1 ounce each) bittersweet or**
  semisweet chocolate
2 **teaspoons shortening, divided**
4 **ounces white chocolate**

To grind hazelnuts, place in food processor or blender. Process until thoroughly ground with a dry, not pasty, texture.

Preheat oven to 350°F. Lightly grease cookie sheets or line with parchment paper. Melt chocolate chips in top of double boiler over hot, not boiling, water. Remove from heat; cool. Blend flour, sugar, hazelnuts, espresso powder and salt in large bowl. Blend in butter, melted chocolate and vanilla until dough is stiff but smooth. (If dough is too soft to handle, cover and refrigerate until firm.)

Roll out dough, ¼ at a time, to ⅛-inch thickness on lightly floured surface. Cut out with 2-inch scalloped round cutters. Place 2 inches apart on prepared cookie sheets. Bake 8 minutes or until not quite firm. (Cookies should not brown. They will puff up during baking and then fall again.) Remove to wire racks to cool.

Place bittersweet chocolate and 1 teaspoon shortening in small bowl. Place bowl over hot water; stir until chocolate is melted and smooth. Dip cookies, 1 at a time, halfway into bittersweet chocolate. Place on waxed paper; refrigerate until chocolate is set. Repeat melting process with white chocolate. Dip other halves of cookies into white chocolate; refrigerate until set. Store cookies in airtight container in cool place. (If cookies are frozen, chocolate may discolor.)

Makes about 4 dozen cookies

Oatmeal Apple Cookies

1¼ cups firmly packed brown sugar
¾ **Butter Flavor* CRISCO® Stick** *or* ¾ cup
  **Butter Flavor CRISCO® all-vegetable
  shortening plus additional for greasing**
¼ cup milk
1 egg
1½ teaspoons vanilla
1 cup all-purpose flour
1¼ teaspoons ground cinnamon
½ teaspoon salt
¼ teaspoon baking soda
¼ teaspoon ground nutmeg
3 cups quick-cooking oats (not instant or
  old-fashioned), uncooked
1 cup diced peeled apples
¾ cup raisins (optional)
¾ cup coarsely chopped walnuts (optional)

*Butter Flavor Crisco is artificially flavored.

1. Heat oven to 375°F. Grease baking sheet. Place sheets of foil on countertop for cooling cookies.

2. Combine brown sugar, ¾ cup shortening, milk, egg and vanilla in large bowl. Beat at medium speed of electric mixer until well blended.

3. Combine flour, cinnamon, salt, baking soda and nutmeg. Add gradually to creamed mixture at low speed. Mix just until blended. Stir in, one at a time, oats, apples, raisins and nuts with spoon. Drop by rounded tablespoonfuls 2 inches apart onto prepared baking sheet.

4. Bake at 375°F for 13 minutes or until set. *Do not overbake.* Cool 2 minutes on baking sheet. Remove cookies to foil to cool completely.

Makes about 2½ dozen cookies

Fruitcake Cookies

½ cup butter, softened
¾ cup sugar
½ cup milk
1 egg
2 tablespoons orange juice
1 tablespoon vinegar
2 cups all-purpose flour
1 teaspoon baking powder
½ teaspoon baking soda
¼ teaspoon salt
½ cup chopped walnuts
½ cup chopped candied mixed fruit
½ cup raisins
¼ cup chopped dried pineapple
  Powdered sugar

Preheat oven to 350°F. Grease cookie sheets. Beat butter and sugar in large bowl until creamy. Beat in milk, egg, orange juice and vinegar until blended. Mix in flour, baking powder, baking soda and salt. Stir in walnuts, mixed fruit, raisins and pineapple. Drop rounded tablespoonfuls of dough 2 inches apart onto prepared cookie sheets.

Bake 12 to 14 minutes until lightly browned around edges. Cool 2 minutes on cookie sheets. Remove to wire racks; cool completely. Dust with powdered sugar. Store in airtight container.

Makes about 2½ dozen cookies

Choco-Cherry Cookies Supreme

⅔ cup all-purpose flour
½ cup unsweetened cocoa
1½ teaspoons baking powder
½ teaspoon salt
⅓ cup butter, softened
½ cup granulated sugar
½ cup packed light brown sugar
⅓ cup milk
1 large egg
1 teaspoon vanilla
2 cups uncooked quick-cooking or old-fashioned oats
3 ounces white baking bar or white chocolate candy bar, cut into ¼-inch pieces
½ cup candied cherries, cut into halves

1. Preheat oven to 375°F. Lightly grease cookie sheets; set aside.

2. Place flour, cocoa, baking powder and salt in small bowl; stir to combine.

3. Beat butter, granulated sugar and brown sugar in large bowl with electric mixer at medium speed until light and fluffy, scraping down side of bowl once. Beat in milk, egg and vanilla, scraping down side of bowl once. Gradually add flour mixture. Beat at low speed, scraping down side of bowl occasionally.

4. Stir in oats until well blended. Stir in baking bar pieces and cherries.

5. Drop heaping teaspoonfuls of dough 2 inches apart onto prepared cookie sheets.

6. Bake 10 minutes or until set. Let cookies stand on cookie sheets 1 minute. Remove cookies to wire racks; cool completely.

7. Store tightly covered at room temperature or freeze up to 3 months.

Makes about 3 dozen cookies

Pineapple Raisin Jumbles

2 cans (8 ounces each) DOLE® Crushed Pineapple
½ cup margarine, softened
½ cup sugar
1 teaspoon vanilla extract
1 cup all-purpose flour
4 teaspoons grated orange peel
1 cup DOLE® Blanched Slivered Almonds, toasted
1 cup DOLE® Seedless Raisins

• Preheat oven to 350°F. Drain pineapple well, pressing out excess liquid with back of spoon.

• In large bowl, beat margarine and sugar until fluffy. Stir in pineapple and vanilla. Beat in flour and orange peel. Stir in almonds and raisins.

• Drop heaping tablespoons of dough 2 inches apart onto greased cookie sheets.

• Bake 20 to 22 minutes or until firm. Cool on wire racks. *Makes 2 to 2½ dozen cookies*

Choco-Cherry Cookies Supreme

Holiday Fruit Drops

½ cup butter, softened
¾ cup packed brown sugar
1 egg
1¼ cups all-purpose flour
1 teaspoon vanilla
½ teaspoon baking soda
½ teaspoon ground cinnamon
   Pinch salt
1 cup (8 ounces) diced candied pineapple
1 cup (8 ounces) whole red and green
   candied cherries*
8 ounces chopped pitted dates
1 cup (6 ounces) semisweet chocolate chips
½ cup whole hazelnuts*
½ cup pecan halves*
½ cup coarsely chopped walnuts

*The cherries, hazelnuts and pecan halves are not chopped, but left whole.

Preheat oven to 325°F. Lightly grease cookie sheets or line with parchment paper. Cream butter and sugar in large bowl. Beat in egg until light and fluffy. Mix in flour, vanilla, baking soda, cinnamon and salt. Stir in pineapple, cherries, dates, chocolate chips, hazelnuts, pecans and walnuts. Drop dough by rounded teaspoonfuls 2 inches apart onto prepared cookie sheets.

Bake 15 to 20 minutes or until firm and lightly browned around edges. Remove to wire racks to cool completely.

Makes about 8 dozen cookies

Choco-Coco Pecan Crisps

½ cup butter, softened
1 cup packed light brown sugar
1 egg
1 teaspoon vanilla
1½ cups all-purpose flour
⅓ cup unsweetened cocoa
½ teaspoon baking soda
1 cup chopped pecans
1 cup flaked coconut

Cream butter and sugar in large bowl until blended. Beat in egg and vanilla. Combine flour, cocoa, baking soda and pecans in small bowl until well blended. Add to creamed mixture, blending until stiff dough is formed. Sprinkle coconut on work surface. Divide dough into 4 parts. Shape each part into roll, about 1½ inches in diameter; roll in coconut until thickly coated. Wrap in plastic wrap; refrigerate until firm, at least 1 hour or up to 2 weeks. (For longer storage, freeze up to 6 weeks.) Preheat oven to 350°F. Line cookie sheets with parchment paper or leave ungreased. Cut rolls into ⅛-inch-thick slices; place 2 inches apart on cookie sheets. Bake 10 to 13 minutes or until firm but not overly browned. Remove to wire racks to cool.

Makes about 6 dozen cookies

Choco-Coco Pecan Crisps

Florentine Cookies

¼ **cup unsalted butter**
¼ **cup sugar**
 1 **tablespoon heavy or whipping cream**
¼ **cup sliced blanched almonds, finely chopped**
¼ **cup walnuts, finely chopped**
 5 **red candied cherries, finely chopped**
 1 **tablespoon golden or dark raisins, finely chopped**
 1 **tablespoon crystallized ginger, finely chopped**
 1 **tablespoon diced candied lemon peel, finely chopped**
 3 **tablespoons all-purpose flour**
 4 **ounces semisweet chocolate, chopped**

1. Preheat oven to 350°F. Grease 2 large baking sheets.

2. Combine butter, sugar and cream in small, heavy saucepan. Cook, uncovered, over medium heat until sugar dissolves and mixture boils, stirring constantly. Cook and stir 1 minute more; remove from heat. Stir in nuts, fruit, ginger and lemon peel. Add flour; mix well.

3. Spoon heaping teaspoon batter onto prepared baking sheet. Repeat, placing 4 cookies on each baking sheet to allow room for spreading.

4. Bake cookies, 1 baking sheet at a time, 8 to 10 minutes until deep brown. Remove baking sheet from oven to wire rack. (If cookies have spread unevenly, push in edges with metal spatula to round out shape.) Cool cookies 1 minute or until firm enough to remove from sheet, then quickly but carefully remove cookies to wire racks. Cool completely.

5. Repeat with remaining batter. (To prevent cookies from spreading too quickly, allow baking sheets to cool before greasing and spooning batter onto sheets.)

6. Bring water in bottom of double boiler just to a boil; remove from heat. Place chocolate in top of double boiler and place over water. Stir chocolate until melted; immediately remove from water. Let chocolate cool slightly.

7. Line large baking sheet with waxed paper. Turn cookies over; spread chocolate on bottoms. Place cookies, chocolate side up, on prepared baking sheet; let stand until chocolate is almost set. Score chocolate in zig-zag pattern with tines of fork. Let stand until completely set or refrigerate until firm. Serve or store in airtight container in refrigerator.

Makes about 2 dozen cookies

Florentine Cookies

Delightful Cutouts

Holiday Sugar Cookies

- 1 cup butter, softened
- ¾ cup sugar
- 1 egg
- 2 cups all-purpose flour
- 1 teaspoon baking powder
- ¼ teaspoon *each* salt and ground cinnamon
- Colored sprinkles or sugars (optional)

Beat butter and sugar until creamy. Add egg; beat until fluffy. Stir in flour, baking powder, salt and cinnamon until well blended. Form dough into a ball; wrap in plastic wrap and flatten. Refrigerate 2 hours or until firm. Preheat oven to 350°F. Roll out dough, small portion at a time, to ¼-inch thickness on floured surface. Cut out with 3-inch cookie cutters. Decorate with sprinkles or sugar. Place on ungreased cookie sheets. Bake 7 to 9 minutes until edges are browned. Let stand on cookie sheets 1 minute; transfer to wire racks to cool.

Makes about 3 dozen cookies

Yule Tree Namesakes

1 recipe Butter Cookie Dough (recipe
  follows)
1 recipe Cookie Glaze (recipe follows)
  Green food coloring
  Powdered sugar
  Assorted candies
3 packages (12 ounces each) semisweet
  chocolate chips, melted
1 cup flaked coconut, tinted green*

*Tinting coconut: Dilute few drops of food coloring with ½
teaspoon water in large plastic bag. Add 1 to 1⅓ cups flaked
coconut. Close bag and shake well until coconut is evenly coated.
If deeper color is desired, add more diluted food color and shake
again.*

1. Preheat oven to 350°F. Roll dough on floured
surface to ⅛-inch thickness. Cut out cookies using
3- to 4-inch tree-shaped cookie cutter. Place
2 inches apart on ungreased cookie sheets.

2. Bake 12 to 14 minutes until edges begin to
brown. Remove to wire racks; cool completely.

3. Reserve ⅓ cup Cookie Glaze; color remaining
glaze green with food coloring. Place cookies on
wire rack over waxed paper-lined cookie sheet.
Spoon green glaze over cookies.

4. Add 1 to 2 tablespoons powdered sugar to
reserved Cookie Glaze. Spoon into pastry bag fitted
with small writing tip. Pipe names onto trees as
shown in photo. Decorate with assorted candies
as shown. Let stand until glaze is set.

5. Spoon melted chocolate into 1¾-inch baking
cups, filling evenly. Let stand until chocolate is
very thick and partially set. Place trees upright in
chocolate. Sprinkle tinted coconut over chocolate.

Makes 24 place cards

Butter Cookie Dough

¾ cup butter, softened
¼ cup granulated sugar
¼ cup packed light brown sugar
 1 egg yolk
1¾ cups all-purpose flour
¾ teaspoon baking powder
⅛ teaspoon salt

1. Combine butter, granulated sugar, brown sugar
and egg yolk in medium bowl. Add flour, baking
powder and salt; mix well.

2. Cover; refrigerate until firm, about 4 hours or
overnight. *Makes about 2 dozen cookies*

Cookie Glaze

4 cups powdered sugar
4 to 6 tablespoons milk

Combine powdered sugar and enough milk to
make a medium-thick pourable glaze.

Makes about 4 cups glaze

Yule Tree Namesakes

Buttery Almond Cutouts

1 cup butter, softened
1½ cups granulated sugar
¾ cup sour cream
2 eggs
3 teaspoons almond extract, divided
1 teaspoon vanilla
4⅓ cups all-purpose flour
1 teaspoon baking powder
1 teaspoon baking soda
½ teaspoon salt
2 cups powdered sugar
2 tablespoons milk
1 tablespoon light corn syrup
   Food coloring

1. Beat butter and granulated sugar in large bowl until light and fluffy. Add sour cream, eggs, 2 teaspoons almond extract and vanilla; beat until smooth. Add flour, baking powder, baking soda and salt; beat just until well blended.

2. Divide dough into 4 pieces; flatten each piece into disk. Wrap each disk tightly with plastic wrap. Refrigerate at least 3 hours or up to 3 days.

3. Combine powdered sugar, milk, corn syrup and remaining 1 teaspoon almond extract in small bowl; stir until smooth. Cover and refrigerate up to 3 days.

4. Preheat oven to 375°F. Working with 1 disk of dough at a time, roll dough out on floured surface to ¼-inch thickness. Cut dough into desired shapes using 2½-inch cookie cutters. Place about 2 inches apart onto ungreased baking sheets. Bake 7 to 8 minutes or until edges are firm and bottoms are brown. Remove from baking sheets to wire rack to cool.

5. Separate powdered sugar mixture into 3 or 4 batches in small bowls; tint each batch with desired food coloring. Frost cookies.

Makes about 3 dozen cookies

Note: To freeze dough, place wrapped disks in resealable plastic food storage bags. Thaw at room temperature before using. Or, cut out cookies, bake and cool completely. Freeze unglazed cookies for up to 2 months. Thaw and glaze as desired.

Make-Ahead Time: up to 3 days in refrigerator or up to 3 months in freezer
Final Prep Time: 30 minutes

Buttery Almond Cutouts

Peanut Butter Cut-Outs

½ cup **SKIPPY®** Creamy Peanut Butter
6 tablespoons margarine or butter, softened
½ cup packed brown sugar
⅓ cup **KARO®** Light or Dark Corn Syrup
1 egg
2 cups flour, divided
1½ teaspoons baking powder
1 teaspoon cinnamon (optional)
⅛ teaspoon salt

1. In large bowl with mixer at medium speed, beat peanut butter, margarine, brown sugar, corn syrup and egg until smooth. Reduce speed; beat in 1 cup flour, baking powder, cinnamon and salt. With spoon stir in remaining 1 cup flour.

2. Divide dough in half. Between two sheets of waxed paper on large cookie sheets, roll each half of dough ¼ inch thick. Refrigerate until firm, about 1 hour.

3. Preheat oven to 350°F. Remove top piece of waxed paper. With floured cookie cutters, cut dough into shapes. Place on ungreased cookie sheets.

4. Bake 10 minutes or until lightly browned. *Do not overbake.* Let stand on cookie sheets 2 minutes. Remove from cookie sheets; cool completely on wire racks. Reroll dough trimmings and cut additional cookies. Decorate as desired.
Makes about 5 dozen cookies

Note: Use scraps of dough to create details on cookies.

Cinnamon-Chocolate Cutouts

2 squares (1 ounce each) unsweetened chocolate
½ cup butter, softened
1 cup granulated sugar
1 egg
1 teaspoon vanilla
3 cups all-purpose flour
2 teaspoons ground cinnamon
½ teaspoon baking soda
¼ teaspoon salt
½ cup sour cream
White decorating icing

Melt chocolate in top of double boiler over hot, not boiling, water. Remove from heat; cool. Cream butter, melted chocolate, granulated sugar, egg and vanilla in large bowl until light. Combine flour, cinnamon, baking soda and salt in small bowl. Stir into creamed mixture with sour cream until smooth. Cover; refrigerate at least 30 minutes.

Preheat oven to 400°F. Lightly grease cookie sheets or line with parchment paper. Roll out dough, one fourth at a time, ¼ inch thick on lightly floured surface. Cut out with cookie cutters. Place 2 inches apart on prepared cookie sheets. Bake 10 minutes or until lightly browned, but not dark. Remove to wire racks to cool. Decorate cookies with icing.
Makes about 6 dozen cookies

Peanut Butter Cut-Outs

Moravian Spice Crisps

⅓ cup shortening
⅓ cup packed brown sugar
¼ cup unsulfured molasses
¼ cup dark corn syrup
1¾ to 2 cups all-purpose flour
2 teaspoons ground ginger
1¼ teaspoons baking soda
1 teaspoon ground cinnamon
½ teaspoon ground cloves
Powdered sugar

1. Melt shortening in small saucepan over low heat. Remove from heat; stir in brown sugar, molasses and corn syrup. Set aside; cool.

2. Place 1½ cups flour, ginger, baking soda, cinnamon and cloves in large bowl; stir to combine. Beat in shortening mixture. Beat in remaining ¼ cup flour until stiff dough forms.

3. Knead dough on lightly floured surface, adding more flour if too sticky. Form dough into 2 discs; wrap in plastic wrap and refrigerate 30 minutes or until firm.

4. Preheat oven to 350°F. Grease cookie sheets; set aside. Working with 1 disc at a time, roll out dough on lightly floured surface to ¹⁄₁₆-inch thickness.

5. Cut dough with floured 2⅜-inch scalloped cookie cutter. (If dough becomes too soft, refrigerate several minutes before continuing.) Gently press dough trimmings together; reroll and cut out more cookies. Place cookies ½ inch apart on prepared cookie sheets.

6. Bake 8 minutes or until firm and lightly browned. Remove cookies to wire racks; cool completely.

7. Place small strips of cardboard or parchment paper over cookies; dust with sifted powdered sugar. Carefully remove cardboard.

Makes about 6 dozen cookies

Holiday Wreath Cookies

1 package (20 ounces) refrigerated sugar
    cookie dough
2 cups shredded coconut
2 to 3 drops green food color
1 container (16 ounces) French vanilla
    frosting
Green sugar or small cinnamon candies

1. Preheat oven to 350°F. Remove dough from wrapper according to package directions. Divide cookie dough in half (keep half of dough refrigerated until needed). Roll dough out on well-floured surface to ⅛-inch-thick rectangle. Cut with cookie cutters to resemble wreaths. Repeat with remaining half of dough.

2. Place cookies about 2 inches apart on ungreased baking sheets. Bake 7 to 9 minutes or until edges are lightly browned. Remove cookies from baking sheets to wire rack to cool completely.

3. Place coconut in plastic food storage bag. Add food color; seal bag and shake until coconut is evenly colored. Frost cookies and decorate as desired.

Makes about 2 dozen cookies

Moravian Spice Crisps

Star Cookie Christmas Tree

COOKIE DOUGH

2¾ cups flour
1 teaspoon ground ginger
½ teaspoon cinnamon
¼ teaspoon salt
⅔ cup KARO® Light Corn Syrup
½ cup packed brown sugar
6 tablespoons margarine or butter

One 10-inch wooden dowel or chopstick (about ¼-inch in diameter)
One 3- or 4-inch styrofoam ball for base

ICING

¼ cup (½ stick) margarine or butter
3 tablespoons KARO® Light Corn Syrup
1½ cups confectioners' sugar
2 teaspoons milk
1 teaspoon vanilla
Green food color
1 container (3¼-ounce) green crystal sugar
Yellow crystal sugar
Miniature colored candies or red cinnamon candies

1. FOR COOKIE DOUGH: In large bowl, stir flour, ginger, cinnamon and salt. In 1-quart saucepan, combine corn syrup, brown sugar and margarine; stir over medium heat until margarine is melted. Stir into flour mixture until well blended. On waxed paper, press dough into rectangle; divide in half. (Do not refrigerate dough before rolling.)

2. Preheat oven to 350°F. On foil-lined baking sheets roll each dough half to scant ¼ inch thick.

3. With a set of ten graduated star-shaped cookie cutters (or with knife), cut dough into 10 graduated stars. Using the smallest cutter, cut 9 more cookies to use as spacers. Remove dough trimmings and reroll. Arrange stars on ungreased cookie sheets.

4. Bake 10 to 15 minutes or until lightly browned. While cookies are warm, use dowel to make a center hole in each cookie. Cool completely on wire racks.

5. FOR ICING: In small bowl with mixer at medium speed, beat margarine, corn syrup, confectioners' sugar, milk and vanilla until smooth. Tint with green food color.

6. FOR BASE: Cut a 1-inch-thick center slice from styrofoam ball. Insert wooden dowel upright in center of slice.

7. TO ASSEMBLE TREE: Starting with largest cookie, spread stars with frosting and sprinkle with green sugar. Slide star down dowel; top with one unfrosted spacer cookie. Repeat with remaining cookies, stacking on dowel in descending size.

8. Sandwich two small stars together; spread with icing and sprinkle with yellow sugar. Place on edge to form top star. Decorate as desired with candies.

Makes one centerpiece

Star Cookie Christmas Tree

Acknowledgments

**The publisher would like to thank the companies and organizations listed below
for the use of their recipes and photographs
in this publication.**

Bestfoods

Dole Food Company, Inc.

Eagle® Brand

Hershey Foods Corporation

Kraft Foods, Inc.

Nestlé USA, Inc.

PLANTERS® Nuts

The Procter & Gamble Company

Index

METRIC CONVERSION CHART

VOLUME MEASUREMENTS (dry)

$1/8$ teaspoon = 0.5 mL
$1/4$ teaspoon = 1 mL
$1/2$ teaspoon = 2 mL
$3/4$ teaspoon = 4 mL
1 teaspoon = 5 mL
1 tablespoon = 15 mL
2 tablespoons = 30 mL
$1/4$ cup = 60 mL
$1/3$ cup = 75 mL
$1/2$ cup = 125 mL
$2/3$ cup = 150 mL
$3/4$ cup = 175 mL
1 cup = 250 mL
2 cups = 1 pint = 500 mL
3 cups = 750 mL
4 cups = 1 quart = 1 L

VOLUME MEASUREMENTS (fluid)

1 fluid ounce (2 tablespoons) = 30 mL
4 fluid ounces ($1/2$ cup) = 125 mL
8 fluid ounces (1 cup) = 250 mL
12 fluid ounces ($1 1/2$ cups) = 375 mL
16 fluid ounces (2 cups) = 500 mL

WEIGHTS (mass)

$1/2$ ounce = 15 g
1 ounce = 30 g
3 ounces = 90 g
4 ounces = 120 g
8 ounces = 225 g
10 ounces = 285 g
12 ounces = 360 g
16 ounces = 1 pound = 450 g

DIMENSIONS

$1/16$ inch = 2 mm
$1/8$ inch = 3 mm
$1/4$ inch = 6 mm
$1/2$ inch = 1.5 cm
$3/4$ inch = 2 cm
1 inch = 2.5 cm

OVEN TEMPERATURES

250°F = 120°C
275°F = 140°C
300°F = 150°C
325°F = 160°C
350°F = 180°C
375°F = 190°C
400°F = 200°C
425°F = 220°C
450°F = 230°C

BAKING PAN SIZES

Utensil	Size in Inches/Quarts	Metric Volume	Size in Centimeters
Baking or Cake Pan (square or rectangular)	8×8×2	2 L	20×20×5
	9×9×2	2.5 L	23×23×5
	12×8×2	3 L	30×20×5
	13×9×2	3.5 L	33×23×5
Loaf Pan	8×4×3	1.5 L	20×10×7
	9×5×3	2 L	23×13×7
Round Layer Cake Pan	8×1½	1.2 L	20×4
	9×1½	1.5 L	23×4
Pie Plate	8×1¼	750 mL	20×3
	9×1¼	1 L	23×3
Baking Dish or Casserole	1 quart	1 L	—
	1½ quart	1.5 L	—
	2 quart	2 L	—